SOUND INNOVATIONS

ENSEMBLE DEVELOPMENT

Chorales and Warm-up Exercises for Tone, Technique and Rhythm

YOUNG CONCERT BAND

Peter **BOONSHAFT** | Chris **BERNOTAS**

Thank you for making *Sound Innovations Ensemble Development for Young Concert Band* a part of your large ensemble curriculum. With 167 exercises, including more than 100 chorales by some of today's most renowned young band composers, this book will be a valuable resource in helping you grow in your understanding and abilities as an ensemble musician.

An assortment of exercises, grouped by key, are presented in a variety of young band difficulty levels. Where possible, several exercises in the same category are provided to allow variety while accomplishing the goals of that specific type of exercise. You will notice that many exercises and chorales are clearly marked with dynamics, articulations, style and tempo for you to practice those aspects of performance. Other exercises are intentionally left for you or your teacher to determine how best to use them in reaching your performance goals.

Whether you are progressing through exercises to better your technical facility or challenging your musicianship with beautiful chorales, we are confident you will be excited, motivated and inspired by using *Sound Innovations Ensemble Development for Young Concert Band*.

D1276634

© 2016 Alfred Music
Sound Innovations® is a registered trademark of Alfred Music
All Rights Reserved including Public Performance

ISBN-10: 1-4706-3394-9
ISBN-13: 978-1-4706-3394-3

Instrument photos courtesy of Yamaha Corporation of America Band & Orchestral Division

Concert B♭ Major (Your F Major)

1 **LONG TONES**

2 **PASSING THE TONIC**

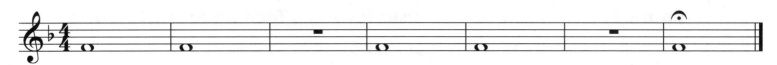

3 **PASSING THE TONIC**

4 **PITCH MATCHING: WOODWIND MOUTHPIECES WITH BAND ACCOMPANIMENT**

5 **SCALE BUILDER**

6 **SCALE BUILDER**

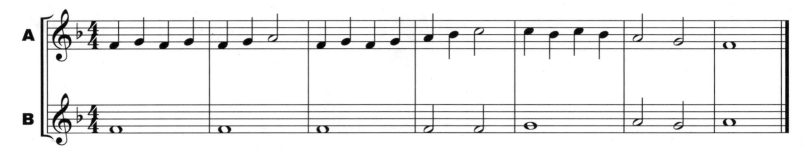

7 EXPANDING INTERVALS: DIATONIC

8 EXPANDING INTERVALS: CHROMATIC

9 INTERVAL BUILDER: DIATONIC INTERVALS

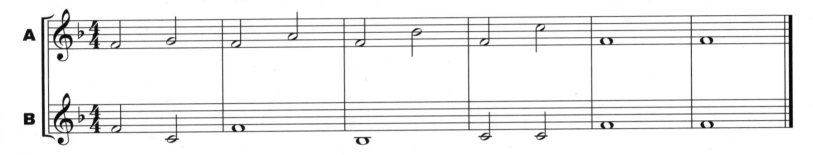

10 INTERVAL BUILDER: PERFECT INTERVALS

11 CHORD BUILDER

12 CHORD BUILDER

13 MOVING CHORD TONES

4

14 DIATONIC HARMONY

15 DIATONIC HARMONY

16 RHYTHMIC SOUNDS

Play the repeated section at least 4 times.

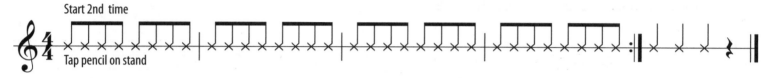

17 RHYTHMIC SUBDIVISION

18 5-NOTE SCALE

19 CANON: 5-NOTE SCALE

20 CANON: 6-NOTE SCALE

21 CANON: 8-NOTE SCALE

22 **CHORALE: 5-NOTE SCALE**

Chris M. Bernotas (ASCAP)

23 **CHORALE: 5-NOTE SCALE**

Chris M. Bernotas (ASCAP)

24 **CHORALE: 6-NOTE SCALE**

Chris M. Bernotas (ASCAP)

25 **CHORALE: 8-NOTE SCALE**

Chris M. Bernotas (ASCAP)

26 **CHORALE: 8-NOTE SCALE**

Chris M. Bernotas (ASCAP)

27 **CHORALE**

Robert Sheldon (ASCAP)

28 **CHORALE**

Moderato

John O'Reilly (ASCAP)

29 **CHORALE**

Ralph Ford (ASCAP)

30 **CHORALE**

Moderately

Michael Story (ASCAP)

31 **CHORALE**

Randall D. Standridge (ASCAP)

32 **CHORALE**

Roland Barrett (ASCAP)

33 **CHORALE**

Slowly

Chris M. Bernotas (ASCAP)

34 **CHORALE**

Rob Grice (ASCAP)

8

8

43 **CHORALE**

Ralph Ford (ASCAP)

44 **CHORALE**

John O'Reilly (ASCAP)

Andante

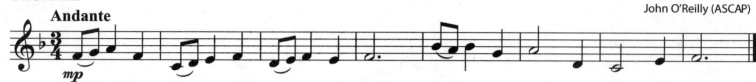

45 **CHORALE**

"Finally the first smells of Summer were in the air. 'Time to plant those strange seeds we found,' she thought."

Jodie Blackshaw (ASCAP)

46 **CHORALE**

Matt Conaway (ASCAP)

Gently flowing

47 **CHORALE**

Randall D. Standridge (ASCAP)

48 **CHORALE**

Robert Sheldon (ASCAP)

49 **CHORALE**

Chris M. Bernotas (ASCAP)

Slowly

50 **CHORALE**

Roland Barrett (ASCAP)

Concert G Minor (Your D Minor)

51 LONG TONES

52 PASSING THE TONIC

53 EXPANDING INTERVALS: DIATONIC

54 INTERVAL BUILDER: DIATONIC INTERVALS

55 CHORD BUILDER

56 DIATONIC HARMONY

57 CHORALE: 5-NOTE SCALE

Chris M. Bernotas (ASCAP)

58 **CHORALE: 8-NOTE SCALE (NATURAL MINOR)**

Chris M. Bernotas (ASCAP)

59 **CHORALE: 8-NOTE SCALE (HARMONIC MINOR)**

Chris M. Bernotas (ASCAP)

60 **CHORALE**

Tyler S. Grant (ASCAP)

61 **CHORALE**

Rob Grice (ASCAP)

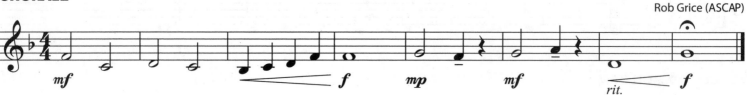

62 **CHORALE**

Robert Sheldon (ASCAP)

63 **CHORALE**

Michael Story (ASCAP)

64 **CHORALE**

Randall D. Standridge (ASCAP)

Concert E♭ Major (Your B♭ Major)

73 | **LONG TONES**

74 | **LONG TONES**

75 | **PASSING THE TONIC**

76 | **PASSING THE TONIC**

77 | **SCALE BUILDER**

78 | **SCALE BUILDER**

13

79 EXPANDING INTERVALS: DIATONIC

80 EXPANDING INTERVALS: CHROMATIC

81 INTERVAL BUILDER: DIATONIC INTERVALS

82 INTERVAL BUILDER: PERFECT INTERVALS

83 CHORD BUILDER

84 CHORD BUILDER

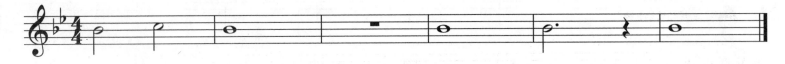

85 MOVING CHORD TONES

86 **DIATONIC HARMONY**

87 **DIATONIC HARMONY**

88 **RHYTHMIC SUBDIVISION**

89 **5-NOTE SCALE**

90 **CANON: 5-NOTE SCALE**

91 **CANON: 6-NOTE SCALE**

92 **CANON: 8-NOTE SCALE**

93 CHORALE: 5-NOTE SCALE

Chris M. Bernotas (ASCAP)

94 CHORALE: 5-NOTE SCALE

Chris M. Bernotas (ASCAP)

95 CHORALE: 6-NOTE SCALE

Chris M. Bernotas (ASCAP)

96 CHORALE: 8-NOTE SCALE

Chris M. Bernotas (ASCAP)

97 CHORALE: 8-NOTE SCALE

Chris M. Bernotas (ASCAP)

98 **CHORALE**

Todd Stalter (ASCAP)

Maestoso

mf

99 **CHORALE**

Michael Story (ASCAP)

Moderately slow

mf

100 **CHORALE**

Rob Grice (ASCAP)

mf   *f*

101 **CHORALE**

Matt Conaway (ASCAP)

Gently

mf

102 **CHORALE**

John O'Reilly (ASCAP)

Moderato

mf

103 **CHORALE**

Scott Watson (BMI)

Moderato

mf   *rit.*

104 **CHORALE**

Roland Barrett (ASCAP)

mf

105 **CHORALE**

Ralph Ford (ASCAP)

Espressivo

mp   *< mf*   *rit.* *p*

Concert C Minor (Your G Minor)

122 **LONG TONES**

123 **PASSING THE TONIC**

124 **EXPANDING INTERVALS: DIATONIC**

125 **INTERVAL BUILDER: DIATONIC INTERVALS**

126 **CHORD BUILDER**

127 **DIATONIC HARMONY**

128 **CHORALE: 5-NOTE SCALE**

Chris M. Bernotas (ASCAP)

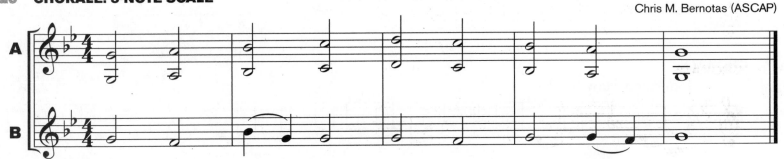

20

Concert F Major (Your C Major)

144 **PASSING THE TONIC**

145 **EXPANDING INTERVALS: CHROMATIC**

146 **CHORD BUILDER**

147 **DIATONIC HARMONY**

148 **CHORALE: 6-NOTE SCALE**

Chris M. Bernotas (ASCAP)

149 **CHORALE**

Rob Grice (ASCAP)

150 **CHORALE**

Ralph Ford (ASCAP)

151 **CHORALE**

Scott Watson (BMI)

152 **CHORALE**

Randall D. Standridge (ASCAP)

153 **CHORALE**

John O'Reilly (ASCAP)

Andante

154 **CHORALE**

Roland Barrett (ASCAP)

155 **CHORALE**

Adapted from Psalm 150, Claude Goudimel
Arranged by Todd Stalter (ASCAP)

Maestoso

Concert D Minor (Your A Minor)

156 **PASSING THE TONIC**

157 **CHORD BUILDER**

158 **DIATONIC HARMONY**

159 **CHORALE: 8-NOTE SCALE (HARMONIC MINOR)**

Chris M. Bernotas (ASCAP)

A

B

160 **CHORALE**

Roland Barrett (ASCAP)

161 **CHORALE**

Robert Sheldon (ASCAP)

162 **CHORALE**

Todd Stalter (ASCAP)

Maestoso

163 **CHORALE**

Scott Watson (BMI)

Adagio

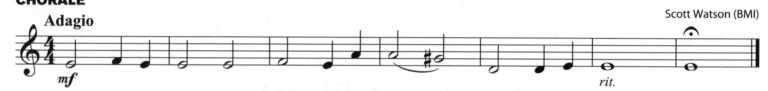

164 **CHORALE**

Michael Story (ASCAP)

Moderately slow

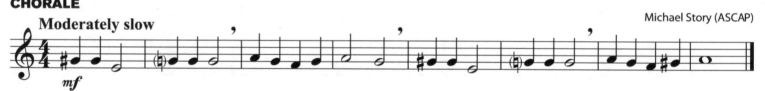

165 **CHORALE**

Ralph Ford (ASCAP)

166 **CHORALE**

Tyler S. Grant (ASCAP)

167 **CHORALE**

Jodie Blackshaw (ASCAP)

"In the darkness all she could hear was the sound of her beating heart. What had she done?"